TOWER HAMLETS PUBLIC LIBRA

C001531029

KU-183-127

Writers Uncovered

BENJAMIN ZEPHANIAH

Vic Parker

Heinemann
LIBRARY

www.heinemann.co.uk/library
Visit our website to find out more information about Heinemann Library books.

To order:
☎ Phone 44 (0) 1865 888066
📄 Send a fax to 44 (0) 1865 314091
💻 Visit the Heinemann bookshop at www.heinemann.co.uk/library to browse our catalogue and order online.

First published in Great Britain by
Heinemann Library, Halley Court, Jordan Hill,
Oxford OX2 8EJ, part of Harcourt Education.

Heinemann is a registered trademark of
Harcourt Education Ltd.

© Harcourt Education Ltd 2006.
First published in paperback in 2007.
The moral right of the proprietor has
been asserted.

All rights reserved. No part of this publication
may be reproduced, stored in a retrieval
system, or transmitted in any form or by any
means, electronic, mechanical, photocopying,
recording, or otherwise, without either the
prior written permission of the publishers or
a licence permitting restricted copying in the
United Kingdom issued by the Copyright
Licensing Agency Ltd, 90 Tottenham Court
Road, London W1T 4LP (www.cla.co.uk).

Editorial: Charlotte Guillain and Dave Harris
Design: Richard Parker and Q2A Solutions
Picture research: Hannah Taylor and Bea Ray
Production: Duncan Gilbert

Originated by Chroma Graphics (O) Pte Ltd.
Printed and bound in China by
  South China Printing Company

10 digit ISBN: 0 431 90630 0 (hardback)
13 digit ISBN: 978 0 431 90630 0

10 digit ISBN: 0 431 90640 8 (paperback)
13 digit ISBN: 978 0 431 90640 9

11 10 09 08 07
10 9 8 7 6 5 4 3 2 1

British Library Cataloguing in Publication Data
Parker, Vic
  Benjamin Zephaniah. – (Writers uncovered)
  821.9'14
A full catalogue record for this book is
available from the British Library.

Acknowledgements
The publishers would like to thank the
following for permission to reproduce
photographs:
Alamy Images p. **17** (Jeff Greenberg); BBC
p. **22**; Benjamin Zephaniah pp. **26, 27, 36,
38, 39**; Bloomsbury pp. **12, 19, 31, 33, 35**;
Camera Press p. **4** (Eamonn McCabe);
Corbis pp. **6** (Hulton-Deutsch Collection),
14 (Michael Nicholson), **20** (Reuters), **8**;
Getty Images pp. **28** (The Image Bank), **7,
11, 21** (Time Life Pictures); Kobal Collection
p. **10** (Warner Bros/Concord); Network
p. **25** (Mike Abrahams); Penguin pp. **23,
29**; Redferns pp. **18** (Mike Prior), **15** (Simon
Ritter); Rex Features pp. **16** (Brendan Beirne),
13 (Everynight Images), **42** (Justin Williams);
Topham Picturepoint p. **9**.

"Who's Who" from *Talking Turkeys* by Benjamin
Zephaniah (Viking, London, 1994). Copyright
© Benjamin Zephaniah 1994. Reproduced by
permission of Penguin Books Ltd.

**Very special thanks to Benjamin Zephaniah for
his assistance in the preparation of this book.**

Every effort has been made to contact
copyright holders of any material reproduced
in this book. Any omissions will be rectified
in subsequent printings if notice is given to
the publishers.

The paper used to print this book comes
from sustainable resources.

CONTENTS

Words appearing in the text in bold, **like this**,
are explained in the glossary.

LONDON BOROUGH TOWER HAMLETS	
C001531029	
HJ	13/08/2007
J821.914	£8.25

A WRITER WITH RHYME AND REASON

I used to think nurses
Were women,
I used to think police
Were men,
I used to think poets
Were boring,
Until I became one of them.
Benjamin Zephaniah

So says Benjamin Zephaniah, one of Britain's best-loved writers of poetry, novels, and plays for young people. He also writes highly-acclaimed poetry for adults, has recorded many albums of music, and is much in demand for radio programmes and presenting on television.

All of Benjamin's work continually challenges our opinions and beliefs about modern-day life, history, politics – everything! If you read one of his books: beware, it can seriously change the way you think. Once you have encountered Zephaniah, there is no going back…

Benjamin has been growing his hair since he was about eleven. He loves his long dreadlocks.

A famous face

Benjamin has been called "Britain's most identifiable poet". He has appeared on television many times, as well as performing on stage all over the world. There are not many poets whose face is as famous as their work.

Benjamin is average height and very fit because he goes running and does martial arts every day. In normal conversation he speaks slowly because he thinks carefully about whatever he says, and he has a gentle, quiet manner. However, when he performs, it is as if somebody has plugged him into the electricity mains and pressed the "on" switch. He fizzes with energy!

FIND OUT MORE...

Here are some of Benjamin's favourites:

Favourite food...	Butterbean stew, chickpeas, sweet potatoes, soya ice cream.
Favourite drink...	Banana juice.
Favourite character...	Frankenstein's monster.
Favourite TV...	Documentaries that let us know the truth.
Favourite film...	Kung fu movies.
Favourite team...	Birmingham's Aston Villa football club, although he lives right next door to West Ham football ground in the East End of London.
Favourite hobbies...	Renovating an old sportscar, collecting rare banknotes, kung fu, jogging, football.
Favourite places...	Jamaica – for its sunshine; India – for its food; Brazil – for its music; Britain – for its **multiculturalism**.

Benjamin Obadiah Iqbal Zephaniah was born in Birmingham on 15 April 1958, just a few minutes before his twin sister. His mother was a nurse from Jamaica and his father was a postman from Barbados. They had left the Caribbean around four years earlier to come to Britain, and had settled in Birmingham.

The inner-city streets full of smoky factories and cramped rows of dingy houses were very different from the sunny lifestyle they had left behind. Money was tight and their home was a tiny **terraced** house with an old-fashioned outside toilet. The house was in an area called Handsworth, where lots of people from Jamaica lived in a close community. As a small child, Benjamin was surrounded by friendly faces, he ate tasty Jamaican food, and he heard a style of Jamaican music called **reggae**.

People from the West Indies first came to Britain on a ship called the *Empire Windrush*, which arrived in June 1948.

FIND OUT MORE...

During World War I (1914–1918) and World War II (1939–1945), so many people were killed that Britain was very short of workers. The government invited people from parts of the old **British Empire** to come and work. Thousands came, from places including the Caribbean and India. Many of these had fought bravely for Britain during the wars, but most British people did not like the arrival of so many foreigners. This led to racial **prejudice** and violence, which grew rapidly over the years.

A childhood of rhythm and rhyme

Benjamin and his twin sister became the eldest of nine Zephaniah children altogether. They had a big family in the Caribbean too, and Benjamin visited them several times when he was growing up.

From a very early age, Benjamin loved how music, words and rhythm were a huge part of Jamaican people's life. Everyone sang and danced to reggae music. Adults knew lots of stories and rhymes that they enjoyed telling aloud. Benjamin's mother even passed on her cooking recipes in rhyme.

Benjamin's parents sometimes worried about him, because he preferred sitting quietly on his own to playing with toys. But Benjamin liked nothing better than to play with word games, rhythms, and rhymes inside his head.

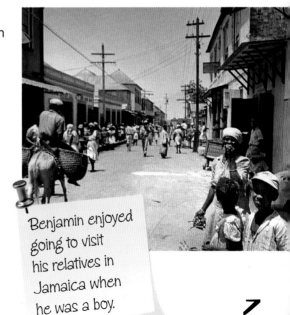

Benjamin enjoyed going to visit his relatives in Jamaica when he was a boy.

7

Suddenly an outsider

When Benjamin was five, the family moved to a different part of Birmingham called Hockley, where most of the people were white. When Benjamin started at school, he and his sister were the only black people there. The headmaster insisted that "every dark person can play cricket", and forced Benjamin into a game even though he had never played before in his life. Benjamin got bowled out on the very first ball, which bounced up fast, hit him on the hand, and broke one of his fingers. Many of the children bullied Benjamin for looking different. Benjamin often spent break-times in a corner of the playground with his only friend – the cat from next door. To make things worse, Benjamin was **dyslexic**, although no one recognised this at the time.

FIND OUT MORE...

Everyone's brain has a right side and a left. The right side controls creative and artistic skills. The left side controls logic and maths skills. Scientists now know that dyslexic people have a slightly larger right side of the brain. This makes them very creative, musical and sporty, but means that they see letters and numbers jumbled up, back to front, or blurry. Dyslexic people are often very intelligent, but need to learn in different ways from non-dyslexic people because reading and writing are problematic. Some famous dyslexic people are: Tom Cruise, the movie star; Princess Beatrice, the Queen's granddaughter; and Richard Branson, the billionaire businessman.

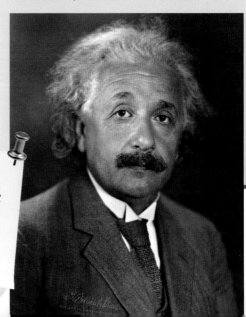

Albert Einstein (1879–1955) was a genius scientist who was also dyslexic.

Many young black children were in a similar situation to Benjamin.

A change for the better

One day, a white boy cycled up behind Benjamin and smashed a brick into his head. After that, his mother moved him to a new school. Benjamin was much happier there. The school was **multiracial** and the teachers were open-minded and creative. In one class, the pupils took turns to pick what they wanted to do. Benjamin would always suggest that they choose a word and see who was best at **improvising** a poem around it. He usually won!

Benjamin had to ask other people to write down his poems because he struggled with writing and reading. When he was eight years old, he entered a poem in a BBC radio competition, pretending it was from "Mr Wilfred Watson of Kidderminster". The BBC **broadcast** Benjamin's poem on the radio and praised Mr Wilfred Watson as a talented poet.

9

Unsettled times

Benjamin's parents often had violent rows. When Benjamin was nine, his mother made the difficult decision to leave the family. She had nowhere to stay and had to leave her children behind, but Benjamin went after her. From then on, they were homeless and moved regularly to **lodgings** in different cities. Benjamin went to fifteen or more schools – one of them for just two days!

However, Benjamin discovered that he had a talent for running when he won his first cross-country race. He loved kung fu movies and began learning the **martial art**. He also gave his first ever public poetry performance at Sunday School when he was eleven years old. It was obvious that Benjamin had a special way with words.

The kung fu movie star Bruce Lee, in the black suit, was one of Benjamin's childhood heroes.

Deep thoughts

Benjamin moved around so much that his only companions were often animals and birds. Benjamin decided he did not want to eat his friends, so he became vegetarian and later **vegan**. He thought about his parents' relationship and decided that women should be treated equally to men. He also wondered why many white people thought they were better than black people. He put all these thoughts and feelings into his poems.

Benjamin admired people who campaigned to change racist attitudes, such as Martin Luther King.

HAVE A GO

HAVE A GO

Try making up a poem on something you care a lot about, like Benjamin does. You could highlight a problem (such as pollution) or praise a solution (such as recycling).

Benjamin's independent thinking often got him into trouble with the teachers. He was sent home many times for being "argumentative", "rebellious", and "uncontrollable". At the age of thirteen, he was excluded permanently from mainstream education and sent away to an **approved school** in Shrewsbury.

Failing at school or school failing Benjamin?

Benjamin's time at the approved school was dreadful. Many years later, he wrote in a story called *Gangsta Rap* about the kind of education that might have helped him – a programme at a type of "positivity centre" which might have given him an opportunity to use his talents and creativity, while also enabling him to get help with writing and maths skills.

Unfortunately, the approved school was nothing like this. It was more like the boys' home he later wrote about in a story called *Refugee Boy* – a hopeless place of dreary everyday routine, bullying, and unhappiness. By the time Benjamin left school, all he had learned was how to get himself deeper into trouble.

INSIDE INFORMATION

In *Refugee Boy*, Alem – the main character – spends one night running away from the boys' home, only to discover in the morning light that he has gone in a big circle and is right back where he started. This is something that actually happened to Benjamin, when he once decided he'd had enough of the approved school and made a bid for freedom!

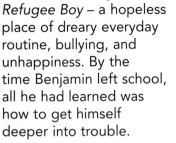

A turning point

Sixteen-year-old Benjamin returned to live in Handsworth, full of frustration and anger. He had no educational qualifications and no job. The only thing Benjamin enjoyed about his life was his poetry. He made up rhymes about the characters he saw around him and performed them at community events.

Benjamin sometimes worked as a reggae DJ and rapped about everything he thought was wrong with life in Britain. Benjamin made people smile and laugh, but he was often in trouble with the police, and finally ended up with a youth offender's prison sentence. In the prison, there was no library or education department. Benjamin was locked up for 23 hours a day with nothing to do other than think. What was he going to do with the rest of his life?

Benjamin was a fan of rappers like Big Youth, who spoke out about life in Jamaica.

By the time Benjamin came out of prison, he was ready to make a new start. Poetry was the one thing he knew how to do – and he wanted to use his talent to make people think about everything that was wrong with the world. But people from his community did not have the opportunities to make a living out of poetry. They became car mechanics or painters and decorators, who sometimes performed poetry as a hobby. Benjamin felt far too passionately about poetry to do it part time.

In 1979, aged 21, Benjamin packed a bag and set off to London. He thought there would be more opportunities for him there. He had no money and had to sleep rough in a car park for three nights before he found somewhere to stay. Nothing was going to put him off: he was determined to be a poet.

Percy Bysshe Shelley (1792–1822) is one of Benjamin's all-time favourite poets.

A purpose for poetry

The only poets most people have heard of are dead white men, such as Shakespeare and Wordsworth. Many people think that poetry is stuffy and old-fashioned, but Benjamin certainly did not think that the only place for poets and poetry was in the past. He thought that a poet today could be a type of news reporter, letting everyone know about stories that were not on the television or in the papers. It also seemed to Benjamin that performing poetry would be a better way to reach a large audience than expecting people to read it for themselves.

Performance poets from Jamaica have a political, musical style known as dub poetry. This is a famous dub poet named Linton Kwesi Johnson.

INSIDE INFORMATION

Some people think that performance poetry is second-rate to written poetry. In fact, spoken poetry goes back thousands of years, long before people invented writing. Benjamin sees poetry as a big tree with many branches, and one of those branches is performance poetry.

On the rampage

Benjamin poured out angry poetry about everything he thought was unjust in the world: racism, sexism, oppressed people in Africa and other countries, how animals are used for experiments, and how governments spend millions on wars instead of helping people.

Benjamin began performing at student unions, on dancefloors, and at bands' concerts. In those days many social groups, such as **Rastafarians**, and campaigning organisations, such as the Campaign for Nuclear Disarmament (CND), often got people together to hold rallies and protest marches. Benjamin was invited to perform at these events too, and the crowds loved him! His life became an endless, tiring round of performing – but there was nothing like the buzz of hearing a crowd chant along with one of his poems.

Benjamin performed with some young comedians whose work had a political message, including Rik Mayall (shown here), Alexei Sayle, Dawn French, and Jennifer Saunders. They have all since become big television stars.

If you think you have got a "wordy great mind" like Benjamin, watch out for "slam" poetry competitions where you can show everyone your talent and spread your message.

This girl is performing in a rap poetry contest at a festival in Florida.

A poet – it's official!

Benjamin took his poems to publishing companies to see if they could be turned into a book. He was turned down many times, but finally a small company called Page One Books agreed to publish them. Benjamin now had a book with his name on the cover. The book was called *Pen Rhythm*.

Not long afterwards, a television company made a programme all about Benjamin. He was excited because television was the best way to reach large audiences. The programme was broadcast by Channel 4 in 1981, and was called *Pen Rhythm Poet*. People were calling Benjamin a poet, at last!

SPREADING THE WORD

Benjamin soon realised that people saw him as a writer as well as a poet. He was a little embarrassed about this, because he could not write! He decided to go to night school and have another go at learning. He met all sorts of people in his evening class and realised that there is nothing wrong with learning at any age. Best of all, this time he succeeded in getting better at writing and reading.

Making music

Benjamin did not start work on a second book straight away. He thought that music would be a good way to reach large audiences, so in 1982, Benjamin made a short recording called *Dub Ranting*, followed by an entire album a year later called *Rasta*. Now Benjamin was a recording artist as well as a poet.

Benjamin's musical work has since included recording a song with the Wailers, a famous band that previously played with the reggae legend Bob Marley (shown here).

Curtain up

Meanwhile, a theatre group approached Benjamin to see if he had ever thought about writing a play. Benjamin created *Playing the Right Tune*, which the group performed locally and then toured around the country. From then on, as well as writing more books of poetry, Benjamin also wrote plays too.

This collection of Benjamin's poetry was published in 1985.

HAVE A GO

If you want to write a play, here are some things to think about:
- Break up the story into scenes in different settings.
- You could work in time order from the beginning to the end, or you could include "flashback" scenes.
- Your characters might talk to the audience sometimes, or you could have a narrator.
- You can write brief instructions to the actors about how to speak and move around the stage.

Words against war

Benjamin was writing a lot about places devastated by war, and decided that he wanted to find out about the troubles for himself. He flew to Gaza, in the **Middle East**, where Palestinian and Israeli people had long been fighting each other over the land. Benjamin stayed with families on both sides, and also travelled around neighbouring Lebanon, where there was civil war. He witnessed terrible acts of violence, destruction and killing, and was in danger himself many times. When Benjamin returned to Britain, he wrote about everything he had seen in a book called *Rasta Time in Palestine*.

From then on, while Benjamin's book publications, plays, record releases and television appearances increased in Britain, he mostly performed outside Europe. Benjamin did so much travelling that over 21 days in 1991 he performed in every continent!

Benjamin travelled to war zones such as Gaza, so he could use his poetry to tell people about what they were not seeing on television or reading in their newspapers.

Benjamin used his poetic talents to tell the world about the struggles of black South Africans.

Making a difference

One country Benjamin worked hard to tell people about was South Africa. There, white people ruled black people through laws called **apartheid**. The government had thrown a black freedom-fighter, Nelson Mandela, in prison for life. With other campaigners, Benjamin worked tirelessly for change. He recorded a song about Mandela with a legendary band called the Wailers.

Mandela was finally released in 1990, after 27 years in prison, and asked to meet Benjamin. Benjamin hosted a special concert for Mandela in 1996 and visited South Africa at Mandela's invitation. Most importantly, apartheid was eventually abolished and Mandela became President of South Africa.

FIND OUT MORE...

Since the late 1980s, Benjamin has often performed abroad at the invitation of the British Council. This is an organisation which increases understanding between people by spreading knowledge about Britain around the world.

Branching out

Benjamin's creativity continued to grow at an amazing rate. While travelling, publishing books, and recording music, he was often asked to present programmes on television. He also began writing plays not just for the stage but also for the screen, sometimes acting in them himself. Somehow in all this whirl of activity, Benjamin managed to find time to fall in love and get married, to a theatre administrator called Amina who he had met at one of his performances.

HAVE A GO

HAVE A GO

Here are Benjamin's top tips for budding writers:
1) read a lot and listen to poetry
2) spend time thinking and talking about important issues
3) start writing from your own experiences
4) above all, be true and be honest.

Benjamin is a born performer.

Benjamin's first two children's books included poetry about poultry!

Writing for young people

In 1991 Benjamin created his first piece of work for young people rather than adults – a play called *Mickey Tekka*. Not long afterwards, an **editor** approached Benjamin to see if he would also like to write a book of poetry for young people. Benjamin had not really thought about how there might be differences between poetry for children and poetry for adults, but he grew really enthusiastic about the idea.

Benjamin and the publisher tried to recreate the energy of one of Benjamin's performances by designing the type in a lively, energetic way, and using lots of photographs and artwork. The book was called *Talking Turkeys*. It went straight to the top of the children's best-selling books list and stayed there for weeks. Benjamin then wrote another book of poetry for children, *Funky Chickens*, published in 1996.

Novel ideas

In 1997, a different publisher contacted Benjamin to suggest another new direction: writing a novel for young people. At first Benjamin turned the idea down. He says: "I was very scared. I thought a novel was like a mountain, and my intellect wouldn't stretch that far."

One of the reasons Benjamin was nervous was because he had only ever read one novel before: the story of one of his favourite Bruce Lee kung fu films called *Enter the Dragon*. He did not think that he knew enough about novels to be able to write one himself.

The publisher sent Benjamin some modern novels to read, including *Junk* by Melvin Burgess and *The Tulip Touch* by Anne Fine. By the time Benjamin had finished these two, he was itching to start writing his own novel. Once he got going, he did not want to stop. His first young people's novel, *Face*, was published in 1999, and received rave reviews. Now Benjamin could add the word "novelist" to his very long list of achievements! Benjamin's second novel, *Refugee Boy*, followed in 2001. His third novel, *Gangsta Rap*, came out in 2004.

FIND OUT MORE...

Benjamin has read more novels since he became a novelist, but many of his favourite books are **non-fiction**. They include:

- *Islam for Beginners*, which Benjamin thought was perfect to get an understanding of one of the world's main religions.
- *Bloody Valentine* by John Williams, which tells the true story of three men who were convicted of a crime they did not commit.
- Books about language by Noam Chomsky, who is a campaigner for change like Benjamin.
- The *Politically Correct Phrase Book* by Nigel Rees, which contains phrases such as "non-human companion" for "pet". Benjamin finds this book very funny.

Benjamin loves to meet young people to share his ideas and find out what they care about.

INSIDE INFORMATION

Out of all the books of poetry Benjamin has now written for young people, his favourite is *School's Out* (1997). He likes this one best because it is full of **radical** ideas and raw emotion, and lots of parents do not approve of it!

You are the future

Benjamin likes writing for young people because young people's minds are much more open to ideas than adults'. For instance, Benjamin thinks there is a contradiction in the way that many adults are willing to go to war with other countries, and yet they tell children not to fight each other. When he discusses this, adults often can not see anything wrong, but young people understand straight away.

Benjamin does not aim to change your opinions, but to make you think hard and make up your own mind. After all, the future of the world is in your hands!

A brain under strain

Today, Benjamin is so in demand for interviews and appearances on television and radio that it is often difficult for him to find time to write. However, he is still passionate about communicating ideas and making people think, whether through the written word, recording in a studio, or performing live.

Luckily, Benjamin has an excellent memory, so he never forgets the poems he creates in his head. He writes them out **longhand**, and has an assistant who makes sense of his spelling and types everything up on a computer. When Benjamin is writing a novel, he finds it frustrating to break off to go travelling or do other things. He gets totally absorbed by his characters and the story is in his head all the time!

Life is very hectic for Benjamin. He enjoys being busy, but like everyone he needs to rest sometimes!

Benjamin's space

Benjamin's home is in Newham, East London. He loves the multicultural community and gets many ideas from all the people he comes across in the neighbourhood. Benjamin is now divorced and lives on his own in a small terraced house. You might think that a very creative, energetic person like Benjamin would have a messy house, with stuff spilling everywhere, but in fact Benjamin likes to keep everything very tidy and organised.

Benjamin writes in his loft, which has been converted into a study and library. His house has three bedrooms, one of which he uses as an office for his assistant. Downstairs, he has a normal front room, but he has turned the back room into a recording studio, filled with musical instruments and his massive music collection. He has also built his own gym and sauna in the garden. Every morning, Benjamin likes to go for a long run, then do a kung fu workout, and relax in the sauna before he starts the day.

Today Benjamin is a qualified teacher of Tibetan style kung fu.

TALKING TURKEYS

Themes

The **themes** in Benjamin's poems cover a wide range of important issues, including animal rights, bullying, war, prejudice, the environment, and how we are taught to see history. The poems do not always complain; they also proclaim positive messages and suggest solutions or ideals we might aim for. The spirit of the whole collection is summed up by *According to My Mood*, in which Benjamin says that he believes poets should have freedom to say whatever they want.

Forms and rhyme schemes

Talking Turkeys is a hugely enjoyable, lively book of poetry that continually surprises the reader with contrasting poetic forms and rhyme schemes. Sometimes he writes free verse (poetry with no regular rhyme), as in *Fear Not*. Sometimes Benjamin writes blank verse (poetry with no regular rhythm), as in *Food for Thought*. Sometimes he uses familiar poetic forms, such as the limerick *Jude*. Most of the time, however, Benjamin invents his own romping stomping rhythms and rhyme schemes, as in *Once Upon a Time*.

Benjamin sometimes plays with the way words look on the page; *Sunnyside Up* is a poem which relies on how it is laid out on the page for its meaning. Benjamin's subject matter may often be serious, but his skilful, creative use of this wide variety of poetic styles makes the book attention-grabbing and interest-holding.

Language

Benjamin writes the way he talks, so his poetry often does not follow the rules of grammar and spelling. For instance, he says "under me bonnet" instead of "under my bonnet" and "dere's a picture" instead of "there's a picture". This use of language makes Benjamin's poems very personal and direct; it's almost as if you can hear his voice as you read.

It is important to remember that Benjamin creates poems for saying aloud, rather than just reading to yourself, so he often plays around with how words sound and what they mean. If you simply read the poems in your head, you will miss out on some of the fun.

BENJAMIN ZEPHANIAH

TALKING TURKEYS

Benjamin's first poetry book for children was bright, bold, and a best-seller! It was published in 1994.

INSIDE INFORMATION

On the BBC's National Poetry Day in 2002, kids voted *Talking Turkeys* their fifth best poem of all time. Animal rights campaigners also love it!

FACE

The plot

Martin Turner is a fifteen-year-old white boy who lives in the East End of London. He has everything going for him: two great mates, Mark and Matthew, a beautiful girlfriend, Natalie, and he is a talented gymnast and dancer. One night, he makes a bad decision and ends up in a terrible car crash. He is lucky to survive, but his face is severely burned. Life for Martin will never be the same again. With the help of a counsellor, Alan Green, and a boy born with facial disfigurements, Anthony, Martin prepares to return to his everyday routine. Will the changes to Martin's outward appearance mean that he also changes on the inside? And will others see the person behind the mask of scars, or will they take him at "face value"?

A major theme: Prejudice

Benjamin once found himself staring at a man with a badly burnt face. He was ashamed, and explained: "I have been to places where there are no black people and have been stared at myself, so I should have known better. I wondered what prejudices a person with a disfigured face would come across. Was discrimination by face the same as discrimination by race?"

Benjamin explores many types of prejudice in *Face*. Tony the priest sees Martin after his accident as "disabled". Martin himself is racially prejudiced, saying that black people "don't like us". Even the judges in a gymnastics competition cannot open their minds to Eastmoreland School's routine: it does not fit with what they expect.

Natalie is an especially interesting character because she is sure she is not racially prejudiced. She says, "I haven't got black friends, I've just got friends". Yet when she sees three innocent Jamaican girls on the street she describes them as looking "good but dangerous".

Face poses a soul-searching question to the reader: are you really sure you are not prejudiced about anything?

INSIDE INFORMATION

Benjamin did lots of research for this novel, meeting several people with facial disfigurement and looking into surgery and counselling. He used memories of a friend who died in a car crash when he was a teenager as a basis for the central event in the story.

This novel tackles a difficult situation and sensitive issues. It was published in 1999.

REFUGEE BOY

The plot

Fourteen-year-old Alem comes from East Africa, where Ethiopia and Eritrea are locked in a bitter war. Tragically, Alem's family are caught in the middle, because his father is Ethiopian and his mother is Eritrean. Alem is thrilled when his father brings him to London for a few days' holiday. He tries out his English, visits everywhere he has seen in books, and eats "real" spaghetti from Italy! However, Alem wakes one morning to find that his father has returned home to Africa without him. His parents have made the heart-breaking decision that Alem would be safer in Britain, until the troubles are over. Now Alem has to fight another kind of war, battling the authorities to stay in Britain. Luckily, Alem finds he is not all on his own after all.

A major theme: Separation

Many characters in *Refugee Boy* have to deal with separation. Stanley Burton has been separated from his family and placed in a boys' home, with devastating effects. Ruth Fitzgerald still lives with her parents, but feels isolated from them because they give their full attention to the young people they foster. **Asylum** seekers are separated from society by paperwork and procedures, even having their own check-out in the supermarket. Alem's friend, Robert Fern, feels separate from his original identity: Roberto Fernandez from Chile.

Fortunately, several characters are dedicated to working to bring people together, such as Alem's own father. Characters such as Asher are determined to rise above divisions that separate communities; he insists that he is "an Ethiopian that happens to be born in England". Overall, there is a positive message that we can always organise ourselves to stand up for togetherness and understanding.

INSIDE INFORMATION

Benjamin was inspired by two teenagers who had come to Britain to escape a terrible war, but who were being turned down for asylum by the government. He has said: "I always remind myself that each refugee is a person, a person who for some reason has left everything they know and love to find safety in a strange, and sometimes hostile country... I had to write a story that would illustrate the suffering and the struggles that many asylum seekers have to endure."

refugee boy

benjamin zephaniah

Benjamin's second novel shows how politics affects everyone – young people as well as old. It was published in 2001.

From the best-selling author of FACE

33

GANGSTA RAP

The plot

Fifteen-year-old Ray, Tyrone and Prem have had enough of school – and school has had enough of them. Permanently excluded from education, they are offered a final opportunity by head teacher, Mr Lang. He recognises the boys' creativity and talent for music, and gives them the chance to develop their potential in a Social Inclusion programme at the local Positivity Centre. The boys put together a band, the Positive Negatives, which become an almost overnight sensation with a recording contract, a passionate fanbase and a number one record. However, it seems that success comes hand-in-hand with enemies and hatred. A war of words with a rival band soon escalates into a real battle of bullets and guns – can the boys find both the will and the way to stop the situation spiralling out of control?

A major theme: Cooperation

At first, Ray, Tyrone and Prem refuse to cooperate with anyone in authority, whether they deserve respect (such as their teachers), or whether they do not (such as Ray's drunken father). But when the boys and their parents all agree to cooperate with Mr Lang's plan, Ray, Tyrone and Prem are able to turn their negative lives into positives.

The boys run the band as a cooperative, giving an equal share of the profits to their manager and father figure, Marga Man. They learn that they must also work with those they see as their enemies. When the boys eventually talk to rival band, the Western Alliance, and also to the police, they realise they all have more in common than they thought. By cooperating, they find out who their true enemy really is.

Benjamin used his own experience of recording studios and the music industry to come up with some of the scenes and characters in *Gangsta Rap*. The novel was published in 2004.

INSIDE INFORMATION

This is what Benjamin has said about *Gangsta Rap*: "I was fascinated by the amount of young people excluded from school who had loads of talent and who then went on to succeed in their chosen careers, usually creative careers... I also wanted to explore the gun culture... In many inner city areas kids no longer get into scraps... now it's a shooting or at the very least a stabbing... Many people say that teenage boys are not interested in poetry, but rap is simply street poetry... Rap tells it as it is."

PRIZES, PASSIONS, AND PRAISE

Benjamin has been offered all sorts of awards for his work, even though he does not always accept them. He is only happy about receiving an award if he agrees with the organisation behind it and their reasons for giving it to him.

Yes please!

In 1989, Oxford University **shortlisted** Benjamin for the position of Professor of Poetry – the first time a performance poet had ever been considered for this prestigious post. Several universities who admire Benjamin's writing have given him a special award called an **honorary doctorate**. This means that his proper title is now "Dr Benjamin Zephaniah".

Benjamin in a special gown and hat that he wore to receive an honorary doctorate at a graduation ceremony.

Benjamin has also been Creative Writer in Residence at Cambridge University, Writer in Residence at the Africa Arts Collective in Liverpool, and Poet in Residence at the legal offices of a London **barrister**, Michael Mansfield QC. *Face was* shortlisted for three awards including the Children's Book Award 2000, and *Refugee Boy* won the Portsmouth Book Award in 2002.

No thanks!

In 2003, Benjamin turned down an award from the Queen called an OBE – the Order of the British Empire. Although he has nothing against the Queen as a person, Benjamin feels angry when he thinks about the actions of the royal family and the British Empire through history, conquering other people's lands and enslaving black nations. Other people feel the same way and have also turned down awards from the Queen. Benjamin was very outspoken about his reasons and feelings, which caused a commotion.

FIND OUT MORE...

In Britain, the official poet of the royal family and the government is called the Poet Laureate. The Poet Laureate is expected to write about important official events. Benjamin would much rather be a type of "people's laureate", speaking up for communities and individuals. The honour which means the most to Benjamin and his mum is having a ward named after him at Ealing Hospital in London. The ward is for people with mental health problems.

Benjamin cares very much about people who are set back in society in ways like this. He thinks that being creative with poetry and art can help them expess themselves. In 2004, Benjamin opened an art exhibition for people in high security mental health units and prisons.

Actions as well as words

Benjamin has said: "When you become famous, people come to you to join their cause – especially me because I speak out on so many causes." One cause Benjamin is fighting for is to find out what happened when his cousin, Michael Powell, died in police **custody** in 2003. Here are a few of many other causes and groups which Benjamin supports:

- Andrew Lee Jones fund – provides money for legal help for prisoners held abroad on death row
- Comfort Family Care Centre – support for East London black families
- Changing Faces – supports people with facial disfigurement
- Chinese Women's Refuge Group
- Disability Equality in Education
- Haven Distribution – provides books for prisoners
- Irie Dance Company
- Musicworks – a young people's music project
- The Polka Children's Theatre, Wimbledon
- The Vegan Society
- Viva! – supports animal rights and vegetarianism.

Benjamin is a big football fan. He sponsors the Central Park Girls' Football Team in London.

Benjamin sees himself as a political person who does not belong to any one political party, and a spiritual person who does not belong to any one religion.

Educational, revelational, inspirational

Although Benjamin hated most of his school days, he now spends much of his time visiting schools to talk to young people. In fact, he has said that if he was not a poet he would like to be a teacher.

He performs his poetry to get everyone thinking about important issues and he tries to inspire children to read books other than school books. Benjamin believes that if you do not read, you are missing out on knowledge and world-changing ideas, besides a lot of fun. He spreads the message that education is vital, but that not all education involves being good at passing exams.

Benjamin's mum is very proud of her famous son.

Views in the news

When you are a famous author like Benjamin, people called critics write their opinions of your work for newspapers and magazines. These are known as book reviews, and they help readers decide whether to spend their time and money on a story or not. Here's an example of a review for *Funky Chickens*, with some notes on how the critic has put it together. Would it encourage you to read the book?

If you've ever said that poetry is boring, be prepared to swallow your words! *Funky Chickens* is filled with funny, fresh rhymes and raps which will leap around inside your head long after you've stopped reading.

a summary of what kind of book it is

This dynamic book from performance poet Benjamin Zephaniah is the follow-up to his ground-breaking first collection for young people, *Talking Turkeys*. Readers of eight and over sent *Talking Turkeys* strutting straight to the top of the children's bestselling book charts, where *Funky Chickens* is no doubt also headed. Young people adore Benjamin's straight-talking street style, his bouncy rhythms and bold rhymes. They are wowed by the way his poems are presented on the page – the typography moves and grooves along with the rhythm, while photos and artwork interact with the words in an imaginative, thought-provoking way. Most of all, young people appreciate Benjamin's subject matter.

some background on the writer

who the work is aimed at

Funky Chickens is filled with poems which question authority and accepted viewpoints, focusing on issues such as the welfare of the planet, animal rights, and prejudice. While the poetic style and presentation make *Funky Chickens* hugely enjoyable, you also cannot fail to be affected by many serious, inspiring ideas. So if you want an entertaining, laugh-a-minute read which will make you think too, this book is for you. Finally, don't forget that Zephaniah's poetry is meant to be performed, so if the urge takes you, jump up, start rapping, and do that funky chicken!

a little about the book without giving too much away

the critic's opinion on whether it is a good or bad read, with clear reasons why

Why not try writing your own review of a Benjamin Zephaniah book or poem? You could give it to a friend who does not know the piece and see if they go on to read it. Ask them to write a review back, recommending one of their own favourite reads to you. You might discover a great new book, poem, or writer!

Pieces of praise

Here are some critics' opinions about Benjamin's work in general:

"Zephaniah deserves a place in our schools alongside the great poets of history."
Children's Express

"Zephaniah is the reigning king of children's poetry ... his are poems that bounce up from the page and demand to be read, rapped, sung and hip-hopped aloud."
The Independent on Sunday

"This is poetry with attitude."
The Times

Praise for Face:
"A strongly plotted story for teenagers, expertly constructed."
The Times Educational Supplement

Praise for Gangsta Rap:
"Not for a long time have I read a book with such a 'pick me up again' factor."
The Independent on Sunday

"A brilliant first novel."
The Guardian

Praise for Refugee Boy:
"[This] deeply moving novel shows Zephaniah's talent at handling big subjects and making them manageable without diluting their intensity."
The Times

LONG LIVE BENJAMIN ZEPHANIAH!

Today, Benjamin loves travelling, but still thinks that Britain is a great place to live. He believes it is one of the few countries which truly aims to have free speech, and which would allow a Rastafarian like himself, who was thrown out of school and who constantly criticizes the **authorities**, to become its representative. However, Benjamin thinks changes are needed to improve our lives. He feels very strongly that together we can make the world a better place for everyone.

Future plans

There will always be an endless supply of ideas and issues for Benjamin to write poems and novels about. He will always feel that it is his duty as a poet to find out the truth and shout it from the rooftops. One of the things that would make Benjamin happiest is to think that he has inspired you to do the same.

If you feel the urge, jump up and start rapping like Benjamin!

Writing in focus

Benjamin has millions of fans worldwide. Here is what some of them think about him and his work:

"Benjamin Zephaniah is my hero."

Robbie, age 15, "A Palestinian who happened to be born in the UK."

"Never ever a lend a Zephaniah book to a friend or face facts for sure – you won't be seeing it no more."

Mark, age 14, the United States

"I wish I was an author like Benjamin Zephaniah."

Nishat Aziz, age 7, London

BENJAMIN'S WISH LIST

Hopes... Benjamin would like one day to visit Tibet. The country is very high up, so the air is still clean and unpolluted. However, he is worried that it might be quite difficult being vegan there, because he's heard that Tibetan people eat a lot of yak!

Dreams... Benjamin would love to have the ability to rid the world of war and the power to heal – also to be able to paint and to have his own full-sized gym.

Ambitions... Benjamin does not want to be rich or really famous, because he has got friends who are rich and they are not happy. He just wants to keep doing what he is doing, for as long as possible. One day he might move to a country house in the middle of nowhere, where he can go jogging in the fresh air and have animals living around him – but luckily for us, he cannot see himself retiring any time soon.

TIMELINE

1958 Benjamin is born on April 15.

1963 Benjamin's family move to a part of Birmingham called Hockley where most of the people are white. He is bullied.

1967 Benjamin's mother leaves the family, but Benjamin goes after her. They are homeless, moving between lodgings in different cities.

1969 Benjamin gives his first ever public poetry performance at Sunday school, aged 11. He is also good at running and kung fu.

1971 Aged 13, Benjamin is sent away to approved school.

1974 Aged 16, Benjamin finishes at the approved school and returns to Birmingham to live in Handsworth. He has no qualifications or job.

1976 Benjamin is sent to prison. He decides that he is going to change the direction of his life by using his talent for poetry.

1979 Aged 21, Benjamin moves from Birmingham to London to try to make a career as a poet.

1980 Benjamin's first poetry book, *Pen Rhythm*, is published by Page One Books.

1981 A television programme is broadcast about Benjamin on Channel 4, called *Pen Rhythm Poet*.

1982 Benjamin makes his first recording, called *Dub Ranting*. He starts travelling abroad to troubled countries.

1985 Benjamin's second poetry collection, *The Dread Affair*, is published. Benjamin writes his first play: *Playing the Right Tune*.

1986 Benjamin releases a recording called *Free South Africa*.

1987 Benjamin writes two plays: *Job Rocking* and *Delirium*. He appears in the Channel 4 film, *Didn't you Kill My Brother?*

1988 Benjamin starts performing abroad at the invitation of the British Council.
He is shortlisted for a Fellowship at Cambridge University.
Ealing Hospital names a ward after Benjamin.

1989 Benjamin is shortlisted for the position of Professor of Poetry at Oxford University.

1990 *Rasta Time in Palestine* (for adults) is published.
Black freedom-fighter Nelson Mandela is released from prison in South Africa.

1991 Benjamin writes his first work for young people, a play called *Mickey Tekka*.
Benjamin writes and acts in his first television play, called *Dread Poets' Society*, which is shown by the BBC.

1993 Benjamin writes and presents *Crossing the Tracks* on television, which later wins the Race in Media Award.

1994 *Talking Turkeys* is published.
Nelson Mandela is elected the first black president of South Africa.

1996 *Funky Chickens* is published.
Benjamin hosts a special concert at the Albert Hall in London in honour of Nelson Mandela.

1997 A publisher suggests to Benjamin that he should try writing a novel for young people.
School's Out: Poems Not for School is published.

1998 The University of North London awards Benjamin an honorary doctorate in recognition of his work.
The government asks Benjamin to be a member of a panel to advise on how music and art should be taught in schools.
Benjamin's play, *Hurricane Dub*, is one of the winners of the BBC Young Playwrights' Festival Award.

1999 *Face* is published. It is shortlisted for three awards, including the Children's Book Award.
The University of Central England makes Benjamin an honorary Doctor of Letters.

2000 A collection of poems for young people called *Wicked World!* is published.

2001 *Refugee Boy* is published. It later wins the Portsmouth Book Award.

2002 The University of Staffordshire makes Benjamin an honorary Doctor of the University.

2003 Benjamin is offered an OBE but turns it down.
He broadcasts *Rasta History* and *Home Truths* on BBC Radio 4.

2004 *Gangsta Rap* is published.
Chambers' Primary Rhyming Dictionary is published.
Benjamin co-hosts the BBC Radio 3 World Music Awards Poll Winners' Concert at Edinburgh's Usher Hall.

FURTHER RESOURCES

More books to read

Benjamin Zephaniah: A Profile, Verna Wilkins (Tamarind Books, 2002)

Chambers Rhyming Dictionary, Benjamin Zephaniah (Chambers, 2003)

We Are Britain!, Benjamin Zephaniah (Frances Lincoln, 2004)

Audiobooks

Versions of much of Benjamin's work are available as audiobooks on CD and cassette, including:

Funky Turkeys (Audiobook and Music Company, 1997)

Wicked World (Penguin, 2000)

Websites

Benjamin's personal website:
www.benjaminzephaniah.com

Find out more about the Michael Powell Campaign:
www.mikeypowell-campaign.org.uk

You can find out all about modern poetry and events at:
www.poetrysociety.org.uk

A site all about books for young people:
www.booktrusted.co.uk

Disclaimer

All the internet addresses (URLs) given in this book were valid at the time of going to press. However, due to the dynamic nature of the Internet, some addresses may have changed, or sites may have ceased to exist since publication. While the author and publishers regret any inconvenience this may cause readers, no responsibility for any such changes can be accepted by either the author or the publishers.

apartheid   laws separating different racial groups in South Africa, which gave power to white people over black people

approved school   special type of school where difficult pupils were taken to live and be taught

asylum   protection given to somebody. An asylum seeker is someone who may have left their own country to find safety.

authorities   organizations who have power and control, such as the government

barrister   person who practises law

British Empire   term used to describe the large group of countries that used to be ruled by Britain

broadcast   transmit by radio or television

custody   protective care

dyslexic   person with an inherited condition that makes it extremely difficult to read, write, and spell

editor   person in a publishing company who oversees the words of a book

honorary doctorate   award given by a university to someone whose achievements they admire

improvise   create something without preparation

lodging   place someone lives in but does not own

longhand   writing on paper with a pen or pencil rather than typing

martial art   method of fighting that has developed as an art form, such as Kung Fu, karate, and judo

Middle East   area made up of countries in southwest Asia and northern Africa, including the Arabian peninsula

multiculturalism   involving people from many different cultures

multiracial   involving people of different races

non-fiction   information books containing facts, rather than made-up stories

prejudice   opinion formed about someone or something without reason, knowledge, or experience

radical   extreme views, often favouring sweeping change

Rastafarian   religious movement which originated in Jamaica

reggae   Afro-Caribbean style of music developed in Jamaica, often linked to Rastafarianism

shortlist   final list of candidates for an award, from which the winner is selected

terrace   row of houses joined together side-by-side

theme   idea explored in detail by an author

vegan   very strict vegetarian who eats no animal products, including eggs and milk

INDEX